A message to my readers;

This book is an introduction of love through my eyes. A poetic depiction of love in simple form. May children, adults, and lovers of all kinds be able to relate to my words. May you be ignited to pass my words along on conscious faith that it'll make the world a loving place.

To whom I acknowledge and dedicate this book to:

One of my many flaws includes the arrogance that I can take the world on alone. That is false by a significant count. Without these people this book wouldn't have existed. Their guidance, patience, & faith in me traveled far to get to this point. For that I thank you all, for that I love you all.

To God, who forever teaches me lessons, molds me and digs inside my inner being to not only be a better person, but have the inner strength, the courage to pay it forward & share my talent with the world. I praise you and continue to ask for your tutelage.

To my parents and grandmother, who taught me work ethic, respect, and had immeasurable patience with me. I love you & hope I have made you proud.

To my sister, who voyages the world in search of exploration, new ground, and self-kinship. May life be good to you, may your adventures inspire you, and I hope to be someone you can seek in any capacity.

To Krentz Sainte & Wilner Pierre, two men who have proven to be brothers and the closest versions of myself. Whether it was late night misbehavior, or early morning productive talks, it all mattered to me. I am grateful for it all, much love and I thank you both.

To Jennifer Melendez, a friend who disappears on me often but is never forgotten, you were the first friend I discussed love with when I crushed on a "certain someone". You were also the first that encouraged me to post "A conversation with love" on Facebook and told me to keep writing. Though you may not realize this, you were the first introduction to how to treat women as a friend and lover. Through mannerism, class, and above all respect. Be well.

To Cece Lebron, I laugh as I write this because you were one of my first fans/editors. Consistent Myspace messages of poems, annoying you for insight of what worked and what didn't. Wherever you are in the world, I hope all is the best.

To Ms. Gross, my 7th grade English teacher at Olney Elementary. Most do not know this but before high school I was memorable for all the wrong reasons. But there was little Ol' Ms. Gross who saw past my tormenting behavior and was the first to tell me I had talent, as you can see I've used my talent well. Thank you.

To Ms. Brooks, my 9th grade English teacher of the Philadelphia Military Academy. Thank you for telling me not to be a lawyer. Good call there. You made English an easy subject to roam, I will never forget the 97 I received in your class which pedestalled the belief that I was academically capable of anything. Thank you.

To "Miss/Mrs." Emilie Frechie, my 10th and 12th grade English teacher of the Philadelphia Military Academy. I write your full name because it brings back memories of you grading my notebook and I would put arrows indicating you go to the next page, "Next page Emilie". Miss Frechie, you by far were the most influential and most dedicated teacher invested in not only my talent but my future. What may be was a brisk moment of guidance for you, transcended into faith in myself, and a career. I'm forever indebted.

To my creative writing teachers at Temple University, you molded my raw talent into crisp, polished, artwork. I am grateful and still in awe. The program at Temple University, nurtured my skill until I was published. Thank you; continue bringing in the new generation with grace and prestige.

To Alex Elle, who I consider to be the mirror of my creative soul. Author of influential and motivational words, mother, lover, & friend. I thank you for your kindness, bravery, and blueprint you've put in place for artist like me.

To my publishing and marketing team, lord knows this book should have been released but the patience that was shown, the care, and attention to detail that was given speaks volumes to me. I thank you.

To fellow artist, don't dare give up, continue to inspire. I look at you all and still feel I can be better every day. Share your talent, change the world.

To Pura Sangre, my first kinfolk, at 16 you all opened my eyes to the world. Took me away from comfortable and expanded my horizon. We took chances, made mistakes, and taught me the world is our canvas, it's ours to create in. I love you all and wish you nothing but blessings.

To the mother of my child who at this point is the only woman I've experienced real love with. Our story has ended and people still listen in awe at our high points. You will always be memorable, for the support of this book, and the journey we shared. For that I am grateful.

And finally; the person I dedicate everything I deem valuable to, my beautiful daughter; Bella Marie Roseau. My darling, you were born in a time of prime love and adoration. There is nothing I want more for you then to be respected, secured, and loved by someone you deem worthy of your heart. Be patient with love, be understanding, and forgiving. I dedicate this book to you and wish you nothing but peace, happiness, and fulfillment.

<u>Entry #1</u>

Q&A

If love was a gender, what would it be?

If love had an enemy, would it fight back?

If love had eyes, what would it see?

If love had hands, who would it touch?

If love took a breath, how would it sound?

If love had ears, who would it listen to?

If love had a heart, who would it love?

<u>*Entry #2*</u>

Untitled

Rivers flowing in different patterns
Flowers growing as if something
casual
Winds calm, a chance to think
Sunlight dead, considered extinct
Leaves falling, grass fading
Beginning to see signs of explaining.
Sun stays set, no cause for change
As silence moves the air
Clouds begin to tear,
It's obvious to the earth
Heaven meets hell here.

<u>*Entry # 3*</u>

Forgiveness

Feelings of desperation, wanting
acceptance.
Your opinion is all that matters
Your attention is all I'm after.
Time is what you need
Slowing down is what must happen.
Sorrow on the inside, tears deeming
count
Our past seemingly the current
mount.
We're redeeming under close eyes,
Pleading with consistency,
Mourning for intimacy.
Why won't you come back?
Isn't it time to forgive me?

<u>Entry# 4</u>

What has become?

Clouds are falling
Catch 1 Catch 2
Put it in your pocket
Make sure rain comes out.
As you watch a car accelerate the
limit
Look at yourself and think what's the
gimmick?
Branches still grow on trees,
Birds still chirp to the morning sun
What is the difference?
Has love grown stronger through
generation?
Tension in seconds, misery builds
As I use my eyes to forecast
My diagnosis is that love has lost
thrill.
Corruption over dignity
A popular multiple choice,
Just depends on who's choosing.
While smiles no longer appear
Romance is known to disappear
The tradition of past so illiterate, it's
deemed unclear.

There's dwelling on my negatives
Not recognizing gifts.
Beauty lies in the deformed,
forgotten, and unusual
Even at times rose thorn
consequences.
The key is movement,
acknowledgment and mention
We grab familiar hands, especially
the resented.
The behavior of habit is so strong,
some never break it.
So I ask you this
As theses times continue to carry
higher voltage
Is it you or I that is more repulsive?

<u>Entry #5</u>

Am I him?

Allusions in the heart
Trickery in the mind
Emotions clearly of another kind.
Saying another's line
Showing a false character
Scrambling for the day after.
This is familiar
Clear to be identical
Behavior quite symmetrical.
I am a spirit
Feelings I do not refrain from.
Cold nights are what I see
I affect in another manner
Respect past the physique.
They may aspire for difference
But I am what I see.

Entry #6

Scared

Two hearts not willing to break
Tired of the same routine
Tired of the same mistakes.
Yearning to fall beyond love
Willing to pay attention
Eyes smiling when the other is
mentioned.
Play the villain
Influenced by the negative
But is love the hero?
Passion, courage, and purity
Traits they were blessed with.
Not that they're unwilling
Not that it won't happen
Repeat to yourself
Trust loyalty and admiration
Emotions in the cuff
Love is the one you're most afraid of.

A conversation with love

Love; many have questions, many
need answers.
When asked why the ones who love
with their all get burned,
Love says; because at times they love
the wrong and do not wait their turn.
When asked, do you last an eternity?
Love responds, yes I do
Just believe.
When asked, why do people think
they can love two?
Is this possible, is this true?
Love says, though it is common and
happens often
This is not true; the heart knows
where and who it lies with.
When asked why did you choose the
heart to live?
Why is it there you sleep at night?
Love responds, I believe it's the
strongest of them all
It takes lot of pain and suffering
before it falls

The heart pushes you to dream and
imagine
The heart feels the happiness and
sadness.
Let's not forget it's been there from
the start
Motivates the legs towards the one
they love
Encourages the arms to wrap around
their other
Convinces the lips to kiss their one
and only.
Tells the brain to pay attention
Just like me the heart will make you
cry
Just like me without it you can't
survive.
When asked, why do people never
find you? Why are some still alone?
Love says, they lost the will to fight,
rather be alone at night.
See though I am a pleasure to have
and fall for
I'm not promised to all, I'm not given
as sure.
To receive me is a part of the battle
but to understand me is the war

To some I don't come on time, to
some not as much I should
But when I come, I make sure to
make it good
You work for it because it's not a
privilege, but a gift
And the ones who work the most are
truly deserving.
Love, do you have anything else to
say? Anything else we should know?
Love says, I will bring you pain, I
will bring you tears
But remember I will overpower that
with joy and compassion
With memories and surprises, with
courage and might.
These are emotions greater than
jealousy and spite.
However, you know when I present
you with that one
Care like you would care for no
other.
Laugh as if you were 5 and under
Your job as well as theirs is to make
it through
Let all your fears go, I'll leave you in
good hands
Just promise you'll give me a chance

Chess, Checkers, Cards

The movements you made are more
than similar
Close to relevant but still familiar
Predictable because of our past
Fear for the future
Minds that won't part
Next move clearly left in the dark
Bases exposed, who's got next?
Could lose it all by one false step

Entry #9

Signs of love

Wind blows in your direction not for
the worse, but to sweep you off your
feet
The sun beams on you, not for pain,
but because your brightness can
compete
Temperature drops not to freeze, but
to cool your heart of raging fire
If it wasn't for you the sky wouldn't
be blue
If it weren't for you love birds
wouldn't be in two
You're earth's aspiration your love's
motivation
Simply to me, you're my dedication.

Entry # 10

New old new old

How can I tell you this story is new
when it's been told?
How can I tell you something new
when to me it's old?
How can you try to create a new first
kiss?
How can you call it a first date when
the first one you missed?
How can you say this is the first time
we fell in love?
How can you say you missed what
never was?
Can't blame it on me if your heart
wasn't true
How can you say what's been lost is
forgotten to you?
How can you say our love stopped
running?
When you were the one, who made
sure to stop it

<u>Entry # 11</u>

Faith

Faith in love often plays villain, not
friend
Faith in love is often a game of
pretend
You sit and wait for imagination to
come to life
Faith in love tends to make you pay a
patient price
It brings wonders, creativity, and
ambition
But take heed to knowledge, you
mustn't forget to listen
No chasing, no searching, just an
outcome
Strength is required
Dedication is respected
Faith in love, can anyone catch it?

<u>*Entry # 12*</u>

Prayer to love

In the name of the father son holy
spirit, Amen.
I call on you love to show me strength
Show me kindness, purity, and
assurance
I call on you love
To have love so strong it blooms
flowers
To have love so complicated it takes
me further
I pray to you so I can stand out.
Stand out in romance and creativity
Show that love is beyond promiscuity
I ask for forgiveness for those I've
deceived
Forgiveness to lives I've given no
consideration
I promise to be humble and non-
judging
I promise to accept the one you put
before me
In the name of the father son holy
spirit
Amen.

<u>*Entry # 13*</u>

Stop

Never understood how a person could
just stop talking
Just stop loving, just stop caring, and
stop believing.
Time put in just a waste
The love endured, disrespect to my
face
Warnings coming from different sides
To busy loving you to listen to pride
Giving up was your intention,
destruction your motivation
Love not given a chance to be that
respiration
Hope was thin, loyalty was strong
You always made it clear; here is not
where you belong
Resentment being asked and conjured
Continuously thinking of a new one
beyond her
What do I call it? How do I explain it?
Why even bother with a love so
tainted?

<u>Entry #14</u>

When love fails

You know it, you feel it, you hate it.
The heart aches, the heart moans, the
heart yells
Screams for answers, grips for
breath.
Looks to see who is watching
There's no warning no protocol.
Senses are broken, feelings not heard
from
Calling back to memory what's left
What happened or who has done.
Look what happened how could you
do this
Love I trusted you. Love I believed
in you
Love you failed me, love there's no
way you can have me.

<u>*Entry # 15*</u>

Being the other

You don't know their identity
Their lifestyle, their personality
An alias amongst you, just there for
the pleasure
All you know is the now, not their
next endeavors
Your feelings poured into them like
water in a river
Just the thought of another can make
you stop and quiver
Your attention to them is turned to
the maximum
While their attention keeps going to
the minimum
Sacrifices in the middle sacrifices in
the end
You're the untold tale
A fairy tale to all
No need to blame them
Who told you to fall?

<u>*Entry #16*</u>

First

I seen her, and I couldn't help smile
She lit up my eyes; she brought
rhythm to my heart
From them on I saw no reason to be
apart
Made my moves told a few jokes
I saw no negatives all I saw was pros
She took my hand, told me be mines
forever
Kept that in mind so made you & I
together.
Love so strong how can it be
deceased
Innocence is the cause for our
longevity
My heart and my openness the
reason you fell for me.
Though young of age but old with
wisdom
Nerves present, wisely overridden
We've started so early, nothing but
potential
Loved you beyond
physical, emotional, and mental

<u>Entry # 17</u>

Planet time

That one day. That one person
That one moment where nothing is
hopeless
You're giving your all, it's received
in full
It's not that you've fell in love, it's
with whom.
Sensation from your heart to finger
tips
Sensation from your toes to luscious
lips
Share the same feeling like a stem
and flower
On this day of days, our love will
grow higher

<u>*Entry # 18*</u>

Friendship & Love

Dirt & grass
Sun & sky
Moon & stars
Paint & canvas
Pencil & paper
There's no difference
Piano & keys
Sticks & drums
Ears & sound
Eyes & sight
Tongue & taste
There's no difference
Feet & socks
Legs & pants
Branches & trees
Love & romance
Friendship & love
There's no difference

Battlefield

With waves of music cluttering the
room
Your heart made it easy for a
suffocating doom
Taste of tears hailing down
Confusion & question leaving the
ground
Just as buildings collapse and ideas
reinvent
Pieces of skin looking to mend
Wounds with colors of darkness
Scars of epic stories
Don't know what's here; don't see
what's left for me

Entry # 20

Crime

I don't know her name
Who knows where she came from?
A walking artwork
Who knows if she's done?
Dreams are constant
Fantasies are all around
Images Images Images
Just
Shattering Shattering Shattering
Down
Different paths, different trails
Secrets of her yet to be unveiled
Can't help but think
How
Did I let you get away with this

A letter to love

Dear love,
We need to talk,
The emotions that run inside me are
awfully deep.
Filled in fear, confusion, and
resistance
You've turned my life upside down,
right side up,
Memories that I'll never leave
behind.
I don't know how we lost our
connection, it's quite a mystery.
You've took it so far, that you've lost
all decency.
As I sit here and write to you, I can't
help but get more infuriated
Didn't see why you made me this so
complicated.
Knew you had great ability to
resurrect life
Knew you could heal what's been
broken
Knew nothing would matter if you
stood beside me.

But like a coward you chose to stand
behind me.
Understanding you is a mystery, so
flow with you I do.
Instead of falling in love with the
other I fell in love with you.
Why choose to stay an enigma to
most, when there is so much to do
Stop being modest, don't be timid
Teach them that you are not a spirit
but soulful, compromised of warmth,
comfort and loyalty.
Show that you go beyond
expectations or any predictability
Redeem those who've lost and feel
escaping
I know it's in you
I know you have it
Because the loss of you in the world,
would be more than tragic
I'm not asking as a friend
Just a loyal admirer
Make us believe again, make us
aspire more.

Tic for Tac

You walk, I run
You tear, I cry
You fall, I catch
You speak, I listen
Love love love
You hug, I kiss
You leave, I miss
You hold, I grab
You first, I last
Love love love
You call, I answer
You move, I follow
You lay, I caress
You adore, I worship
Love love love
You wish, I grant
You give, I cherish
You look, I found
You love, I love
Love love love

<u>Entry # 23</u>

You

In different eyes I see you
But with the same heart I love you.
Tales of us down to different
generations.
Depicting our fear
Our souls
Our motives
Our aspirations
Prone to achieve the unbelievable
Destined to capture the unattainable
Loving you with my all
Is truly unmistakable.
Our tears guided on the river of
redemption
The same river of which we long to
cleanse in
Now that we feel love in this great
magnitude
I see no one else I'd rather share this
with, but you.

Entry # 24

Shy

Experience at its lowest
Commitment being struggled for
No words no expressions of how I
adore
What's inside stays in
What's on the out, relives
What's thought is not acted
What's sought is not captured
Continuous game of courage and
virtue
Still stuck on how to approach you

Entry # 25

Excitement

Joys of your essence
Smile for your presence
Memories run vivid
Signs of you timid
Complication seeping through the
ground
Happiness no longer a sound
Fire flowing down the branches
Raising expectations
Nowhere to settle
So exuberant with touch
So rosy by a look
Would've waited forever, no matter
how long it took

<u>Entry # 26</u>

A new

While strength is key
Forgiveness is courage
Persistence and timing is objective.
Playing tricks with time, bring the
advantage
Sickness for fate, cure for
spontaneity.
Ringing bells, booming hearts
Fairy tales and missing parts.
Much to learn much adaption
transcended
Beauty and wisdom mixed so well;
it's complimented
Avalanched emotion
Heated by lava hesitation
What once was dark is now truly
clear

Unattainable

Like a child who lays and dreams up
fantasies
Always left thinking what is left to
be.
The world, its canvas
You its, paintbrush
But to claim the impossible
Remember, there's no rush.
What's different is what intrigues
Because unforsaken and unforeseen
Not in life, not in heaven, nor tale,
nor dream,
Though worshiped it may be.
Complications rest on every corner
and turn
Can never sit and think
Always lessons to be learned.
Impressions much needed
Convincing an image of insult
Up to you, up to love, to choose the
result

<u>*Entry # 28*</u>

For you

For you I will change the face of the
earth
For you I vow my innocence to love
For you my all is not an option
For you I will layout the stars and
watch it
For you, dreams of tomorrow can be
lived today
For you I'll watch the sun stream
away
For you there will be no competition
For you for you
For you

Night

Oh what a beautiful night
On a night of this stature
You feel the breeze of refreshment
Wrapped in the essence of
consistence
Gleaming with faith of love
Oh what a beautiful night
On a night of this stature
Jubilance walks the streets
And music oh music
Plays such a whimsical
Persuasive tone
Oh what a beautiful night
On a night of this stature

<u>*Entry # 30*</u>

Love's funeral

We gather here today to say goodbye
to a dear friend
Love was many things
Forgiving, kind, and even
adventurous
As we lay these flowers on an
immortal soul
Can't help but think what drove love
to this toll
Was it the non-belief?
Was it the unforgiving hearts?
Or
Was it the promiscuous
counterparts?
While this death is a tragic mystery
We must flip the page of its history
A life now living in a loveless world
A world with
No melodies or sonnets
No art no serenades
The beginning of the end
Goodbye my friend

<u>*Entry # 31*</u>

Trickery

Catching my offense on defensive
stand
My heart on the back burner
My primary option a backup plan.
Move swiftly through the wind
We're calm in an inferno
Question; who's turn though?
Step out before the voyage
Lines scripted before the
conversation
Make moves, moves justly
Play with my mind, seduce the
affection
Hit high, burn low, grip fast, kill
slow.

Entry # 32

Confusion

Where to start? Where to begin?
Can't go through this again
Staring at the old station wagon,
Where laughter filled the seats and tears
steamed the windows
Stop sign at the intersect
Which way to go?
Temptation pointing left
Curiosity steering right
Flood rising
Drowning in filth by the sea
Looking for answers, dividing all
dividends
Where lies the quotient?
Abort abort abort
The damage deemed contagious
Thinking what to make of this
Must keep moving
Must stride through this garden of
clarity,
Where vines wrap around the legs and
bleed fear,
Where grass grows so high it impairs the
vision
But yet, but yet
Where do I start where do I begin
I won't go through this again

<u>Entry # 33</u>

Worth

Lost all motivation
Ambition by the gutter
Why continue? Get love by another
Fading all beliefs
Sacrificing all pride
Tearing down all shapes all size
Mistaken if thought, intelligence is
lost
Pushing the limits
Our loss you cause
New to you, old to me
Don't be willing to take the bait
Hope losing me is worth the mistake

<u>*Entry # 34*</u>

Difference

Anger depression regret
Feelings that should've never met
Quiet comfort inside of me
No exit no need why
Happiness is clearly on the other side
Tears for the memories
Graves for the pain
The sun no longer dances on
shameless days
Winds not a whisper
Eyes so weary,
Finally calling to mind what's truly
meant for me

<u>*Entry # 35*</u>

Can't continue

She writes me a letter
Detailed and all
Hesitation to none.
With a flower in hair
Tied a bow around her finger
We scheme on time
Plot on expansion
To art
For religion
Through music
By devotion.
Watch me, watch you
Acknowledging what's left behind
She walks off,
Wipes her face,
The letter she reads
Is now out of place.

<u>Entry #36</u>

Dream

Swimming through clouds of purity
Laying on stars of solitude
Walking a rainbow of impossibility
Loving the thought of invincibility
Dazed by the outlook
Woven in to all concepts
Undermining all prospects
Filling requirements that's not met
A glimpse of time ruled by fantasy
A glimpse of heart carried by
imagination
Dreams meant for dreaming
Not only in sedation

Why not?

Baseball games, stormy nights
Two wrongs, a left, three rights
Constructed horizon manufactured
grass
Keep the energy low, forget the past.
Blink while open pupils
Hold while hands by side
Live during death and suicide.
While walking on a stream of death
waves
Embrace the goddess of evil
Mix the branches with snow
Watch the monkeys put on a show
Eventually is something waiting to
happen
Can have it in your hand
But still not captured

<u>*Entry# 38*</u>

Vow

Warmth of words, context of color
Devotion gratified to one another
No effort of misuses
All left near confusion
Cleared to play while bases loaded
Good to go when lights are holding.
For sick and in health
Through thunder and fire
With wrong and sin
The same will carry from beginning
to end.
A band that symbolizes a circle of life
A ceremony to rejoice a new made
twice
One filled with jewels of learning
Take ignorance to what has been
yearning
Because one another is your religion
It's your clarity, it's your
prescription

<u>*Entry # 39*</u>

Chaos

Take her pawn, play my bishop
King the opportunity, seize the
chance
Watch her fall, play my hand.
Dance to music, sing to this dance
I plan to make you fall again,
Dim light, stretched far and wide
Death is reaching, look inside
Read the signs, understanding the
language
In between time is the
understatement
Charity of stars waved through
traffic
Generosity seems to be her passion.
Slow down the tempo, listen well
This is what you need in order to sell
Sex the mind curve the heart
Play hers then lose your part

<u>Entry # 40</u>

In a living Room

Please the bracelet of charm
Wrap the necklace of comfort
Pearls of night time around her neck
I kiss I caress
Always putting the daytime to test
Earrings to hear the jewelry of seduction
Pierce the virginity of the wound
Light of eyes
Cry of plead
Lullabies, sheep crossing
Increase the pace, enough flipping and
tossing
Paint the wall with yellow
Mix the color with blue
An artwork of green envy, amongst the
two
We yawn; we lay back, reminisce & assist
Look through the pictures analyze and
clip
Curly hair, blue eyes, pretty smile
Never knew one to drive me wild
Dig up treasures of past loves
Jewels, letters, clothing
A promise she told me
Pictures of negatives, brings us in better
lighting
Fall in love a second; time me

Old love

Stuck vividly, repetition of rewind
Changed momentum, feelings of new
mind
Yet carved is the effect
The intention is resurrect
Being lost is the respect
The solution as of yet
Said love was forever
Promises after promises
Caution after yield
What's given is still not sure
Money falling up and out the ground
This is so familiar
Why not listen to this sound?

Love Kingdom

It's been a long time
Never thought I'd return
Where a smile is on every heart
Where the color of the sky isn't you
Where lust is prevailed by friendship
and affection
Longevity of hopeful sights and
minds
Hands that reach with blinds eyes
Mouths that speak,
With adoring kinds
Times that last a second longer
Sounds of careless, heartless
immunity
Each step softer than the last
Imagery of notebook tales
Scents of engaging hearts
Texture of soothing trust
Sounds of longing union
Come one come all to love kingdom

<u>*Entry # 43*</u>

Heavy thirst of you

Bloom your eyes to show your
character
Close your mind to shutter the static
Hula-hoop the sun, a burn were after.
Slide through the mud, grab a hand,
clap it.
Contact with intimidation
Defeat by elimination
All sights all sounds present
correlation
Magnify anthills, zoom out the
scenery
The crave is glue
The quench is addition
No calls no tells
No mentions

<u>*Entry # 44*</u>

A notebook A letter A note

With a breath of temptation clearing
through the forest of dirt and
dishonesty
Time will only tell of the endeavors
good and evil
Rain falls, sky rises
Ground breaks, leaves climbing
No tell of distance
Just story of tales
Searching of what magnitude to
grade this scale
Burn the grass, inhale curiosity
Run from pride, embrace anxiety

Mile of meadow

Daffodils, lilies, and tress
We never try to reach its peak
Fall short, lost the race, its over
Put an end to this incomplete story
Swing through meadows
Slide by ponds
Crawl out of caves
Yell in a sea shell
Sit with Satan, make home hell
Pink clouds purple sun
Sit back close your eyes
Let yellow river run
Saw through mountain
Leave your mark
Look back on it, hit restart

<u>*Entry #46*</u>

Universe my universe

If I could touch a star
I would feel all sensation
The moon would be my guide
Clouds my pillow
Uranus the home away from home
While I sit back and gaze at you
We continue to run the globe
Shredding the tears for rivers and
oceans
Light gas under comets, smoked
grass of evolution.
Into the Milky Way
Our beginning a devastating
conclusion

<u>*Entry # 47*</u>

Sister

From texture to smell
From sight to persona
It's all a beautiful depiction
Generosity you halo
Courage your wings
Losing you as a person knows of no
such things
Though simplicity is what you're
deemed
But charismatic is what you are
Shining Shining Shining
As if an immaculate star
The friendship we share will grow
older with wisdom but younger in
age
Prone to reminisce while settling
through our dying days
While separation is expected and
lives to evolve
We know to be loyal because love is
our cause
On this canvas we call
Yourself

It's collided with grace strength and
kindness
Beauty is blindness
Unique you surpass
Destined to succeed
A spirit to explore
My inner being
My guardian angel
My left to my right
May love, might, and trust, sleep with
you tonight

<u>Entry #48</u>

Queen

Adored, entertained, deserving of a
king
Where do you find such power?
Elegance of mastered natural
charisma
Walks with angels and spirits with
such please.
Though the foot is light and touch is
heavy
Emotions run frequent
Due to memories.
Gods have fallen
A queen stands no chance
There is steps needed to this
dangerous dance.
A waltz by the garden
Foxtrot of construction
Ballroom my way to sacrificial
seduction
Yet where were you, when her heart
went missing?

Parts of you

A woman's body is God's gift
Filled with meaning and uses
Eyes show character
Lips to bait
Smiles that capture in different ways
Ears listen to worries
Arms wrapped around trouble
It's not to be taken advantage of,
It supports you
It carries you
It loves
Never needs you
A tough physique to replicate
One a man cannot duplicate

Unpoetic

To define love, is to define life
Love is art, inspiration
A classic collection of memoirs
Love is private and traditional
Love is faith
Humans are instant creatures with
speed reaction
Show faith to your partner and they
react accordingly
Patience for this spirit
Love has two sides,
Mind and emotion
Put them together, still bad
connection
Miscalculated balance is cause for
that
It's not a shooting star
It's not a lost unicorn
If anything, it's what we're living for

<u>*Entry# 51*</u>

Fall

We laugh as if leaves stay gold all
year
We live as if happiness never
disappears
Ruby red cheeks, white glistening
teeth
Smooth décor & whimsical persona
Young night adventure
Smile in angel wings
Obvious to reality
This blizzard of hand
Needs no commitment

<u>*Entry # 52*</u>

Q&A (P.2)

Though love is not heard
Though love is not seen
Love is very much alive.
Love is nor man no woman
No beast nor creature,
Not devil or angel.
Love fights back with every rose
Heart
&
Friendship
Love feels sadness for those who
don't receive.
Love smiles at two I dos
& the watching of lips
Reading I love you too.
Love sees all
Love is all
Love endures all.
Love be with me forever
Love guide me through these
nights
Love you are my reason for life.

"In life, you're given family in some form, whether it is mom, dad, aunt, uncle, brother, sister, so forth and so forth. They have a job. You also come across friends rather easily, whether it be in the neighborhood, school, work, or just in passing. They have a job. But a lover, that's the hard one, that's the one you choose. It doesn't fall in your lap so easily, let alone work. And when it does work, and at functional form, you have to take on the role of being family, friend, and lover. You're their whole support system, their teacher, their security, even their punching bag. You learn from them, you grow with them, raise a life with them. More than family, more than a best friend, truly in every bit of the word, that is your partner. Do you understand how special that is?"

-*Adler Roseau*

When interviewed and asked, why does love mean so much to you?